DATE DUE		

2-4

FROGS

UNUSUAL ANIMALS

Lynn M. Stone

The Rourke Corporation, Inc.
Vero Beach, Florida 32964

Edited by Sandra A. Robinson

PHOTO CREDITS

© James P. Rowan: cover, pages 13, 17, 21; © Lynn M. Stone: title page, pages 4, 7, 8, 10; © Breck Kent: pages 12, 15, 18.

Library of Congress Cataloging-in-Publication Data

Stone, Lynn M.
  Frogs / by Lynn M. Stone.
    p.   cm. — (Unusual animals)
  Includes index.
  Summary: Discusses the physical characteristics, homes, and behavior of several unusual frogs.
    ISBN 0-86593-279-4
    1. Frogs—Juvenile literature. [1. Frogs.] I. Title. II. Series: Stone, Lynn M. Unusual animals.
QL668.E2S84   1993
597.8'9—dc20
                                                     93-7460
                                                        CIP
                                                        AC

TABLE OF CONTENTS

THE UNUSUAL FROGS

The frogs you know best leap and swim. But some of the world's 3,400 known kinds, or **species,** of frogs do more than just leap and swim.

For example, many species of frogs climb trees. Some even "parachute" from the treetops to the ground. Other frogs wear beautiful colors but produce deadly poison. Frogs are among the most interesting and unusual creatures in the animal kingdom.

*Climbing comes naturally
   to the barking tree frog*

TREE FROGS

Tree frogs spend part of their lives in trees or shrubs. Most tree frogs are much smaller than the familiar bullfrogs and green frogs of North American ponds.

Tree frogs, also known as tree toads, have slim waists and log limbs. They have wide, sticky **discs** at the tips of their toes to help them climb and leap among the branches and leaves.

The coquí tree frogs of Puerto Rico spend the night in trees. Each morning, in a "rain" of frogs, they leap to the ground.

Sticky toes give this green tree frog a sure grip

FROG CAMOUFLAGE

Sometimes tree frogs seem to disappear. The color of a tree frog usually looks like the color of its surroundings. This allows the tree frog to be **camouflaged**—hidden by its color—even when it is in plain sight!

Depending on where it is, the same tree frog may be gray at one time and green at another. It can also change from a single color to a pattern of markings.

The pine woods tree frog's colors match its environment

TREE FROGS OF NORTH AMERICA

Spring peepers are some of the best-known tree frogs in North America. At least their *calls* are well-known. Like other tree frogs, spring peepers are often heard but rarely seen.

Various kinds of tree frogs live throughout much of wooded North America, especially in wet, warm regions. The little grass frog, less than 1 inch long, is the smallest of the group. The Cuban tree frog, which grows to be 5 inches, is the largest.

The Cuban tree frog is the family giant

The brilliant red-eyed tree frog of Costa Rica

White's tree frog is a native of Australia

POISON-ARROW FROGS

The little poison-arrow frogs of Central and South America show off some of the animal world's brilliant colors. Underneath the beautiful skin, however, they produce a poison that can be deadly to **predators,** animals that catch and eat them. The bright coloring may be nature's way of warning predators to beware.

Poison-arrow frogs live on soggy ground and among roots and fallen leaves in the rain forests.

The poison-arrow frog's beauty is only skin-deep

FROG POISON

Long ago, the native people of Central and South America learned to use the poison-arrow frogs' poison, or **venom.** The natives dip their hunting darts and arrows in the poison. That makes the sharp points extremely deadly.

A poison-arrow frog drips venom through its skin when it is hurt, too cold—or too hot. The natives collect venom by slowly roasting a frog over fire. The venom from just one animal can poison 50 darts!

South American natives roast poison-arrow frogs for their venom

PREDATORS AND PREY

As predators themselves, frogs eat mostly insects. Some species eat other small animals, too.

A frog catches its **prey**—the animal it is hunting—on its long, sticky tongue. A frog can flick its tongue at an insect very fast.

Except for the poison-arrow frogs, frogs are prey for many birds and animals. Even scorpions and tarantulas dine on little frogs.

Even a little frog is a mouthful for a ribbon snake

NOISY FROGS

Male frogs are noisy creatures. Their choruses of whistles, peeps, grunts, barks and other calls can be nearly deafening on a wet, still night.

Male frogs call females with the help of **vocal sacs** under their throats. The frog fills the balloonlike vocal sac with air and vibrates it to make sound.

In the southeastern United States, green and squirrel tree frogs often call just before and during rain storms. They have earned the nickname "rain frogs."

A spring peeper calling for a mate is a sure sign of winter's end

BABY FROGS

Frogs belong to a group of soft, moist-skinned animals called **amphibians.** In most cases, they spend their first days of life in water. Then they become air-breathing, land-based animals.

Most frogs lay their eggs in jellylike masses in ponds. Baby frogs, known as tadpoles, emerge from the eggs. As they grow, the tadpoles develop legs and lose their tails. Within a few weeks or months, they change into adult frogs and leave the pond.

Glossary

amphibian (am FIB ee en) — any of a group of soft, moist-skinned animals that are born in water but become air-breathing creatures as adults; frogs, toads, salamanders and their relatives

camouflage (KAM o flahj) — to hide by matching an animal's color to its surroundings

disc (DIHSK) — a flat, round object

predator (PRED uh tor) — an animal that kills other animals for food

prey (PRAY) — an animal that is hunted for food by another animal

species (SPEE sheez) — within a group of closely-related animals, such as tree frogs, one certain kind or type (*green* tree frog)

venom (VEN uhm) — poison produced by certain animals, such as the poison-arrow frogs of Central and South America

vocal sac (VO kul SAHK) — a balloonlike structure under a frog's throat that can be filled with air to produce sound

INDEX